Pan

S. Ellan

Copyediting & cover design: SSGC Edits (ssgcedits.net)

ISBN: 9798579195234

Self-published

To roamers

Contents

Praises

Lulling Piper

Mist of surprise.
Peace be upon your head,
Fireflies on your path.

Hard edges, soft middle;
Coarse voice, pure eyes;
Short stays, endless heart;
Lives only to please,
Pleased only by life.

With your blessing, my dear, go I
Forever into the pines;
With your blessing, my dear, dive I
Forever into the lines;
Blessings, blessings, you and I
Forever midnight drives.

Three

We write in whosever tone of whatever colour suits your
eyes

To satisfy the urge to tell you

Of dancing in your hometown, of foreign trees,

And of the shooting star that blessed the harvest.

You are the only one we want to write to

And the one we cannot call upon,

Except silently,

Since you speak the tongue of trees,

And know what the moon only knows.

Child of the edge, taken in by the mountain,

May your path be ever covered in soft grass;

May your road stretch endlessly onward;

May the highland flowers bless you forever.

Trails

At the top all is golden;

Leaves respond to sea waves;

Tree trunks, to ship masts.

Under the burning sun,

Where the earth is red,

The hills scream out their strength;

Sunflowers dance in the light.

Under the pine trees,

The sun never reaches the ground —

Only the campfire comforts the fools.

But the river flows in the shade.

Under the branches,

On the path to the water,

Roamers sense you.

Green hills sing to lonely hearts and crowded heads;

There blows the breath of all living things.

Let it burst our lungs.

2.30 AM

Forest eyes,

Summer lasts till December

When you dance on the hills,

When you paint on riverbanks

And splash laughter onto the lake.

You face the world with lies,

Pour wilderness into our boots,

Open trails.

Spring blooms in January,

Since you jumped into the ice

And filled the woods with song.

You break the world with rhymes,

Pull over for wildflowers,

Set time.

Beholder

Fireflies look brighter

From our favourite tree.

They fly above you,

Go where no one can follow,

Rival the stars and aim higher.

We know what it's like to never stop;

We know the pain they are flying from.

No one can hold them.

But, as we sit on this very branch

And return to it from time to time,

So could they land on your hair

And return to you.

Nothing I

The mountain man,

Smoking outside my door

For the square to see,

Knows nothing of the tides.

But his hands built the fireplace,

Where flames and waves dance,

Fogging up the greenhouse.

The master light,

Comes every three weeks

To tell lies and do laundry,

Knows all that can be known;

And ends the sea storm,

Leaving the hills, the cold wind

Burning impossibly slow.

Mountain Myth

Spot the free,

Wearing the forest under a new shirt,

Laughing at the walls,

Inviting others into the havoc,

Saving them

and smiling;

Only trees and foxes

May know the abyss.

Spot the wild,

Thriving off strange looks, smoke, and speed,

Showing up at noon with tired eyes,

Showing up at night with wired eyes,

Seeing the hip goddess of main street

Ache for the paper-hat fool.

Only the silence,

The untraceable thread of inactivity,

May know our circling dance,

Our eternal parted roading,

The restlessness.

Spot the Teacher of the Year '16,

Disaster roadster,
God of the forest.

Let the fire expose the trees,
Let the trees remind you of being still,
Let the stillness wrap you in ribbons.

To remain wild, we must burn —
The only rule you wrote
On the steps of your Earth-old dance.

Healer

Father of the forest,
Saviour of the seeds,
For you sing man and flute;
To you, we walk eternally.

To meet you on the delta;
To meet you by the bay;
To stay on the hills of peace.

Pan,
Pretend until we're dancing.

Mountain Origin

Soft, softer,

Gentle silence,

Blurry smiles.

In the sun, all is in sight;

In the fog, we live free.

Our roses bloom cold;

Our roses bloom faint.

Soft, softer

Sweet mist,

Green pines.

On the wall, silence we paint;

On the hills, live our kisses.

Our stillness grows loud;

Our stillness grows tall.

Hallowed

The hills put their spirit in you.
Tired of standing silent,
They use your voice to sing.

Is it your eyes or theirs,
That watch, haunt, and call?
Is the tune we walk to
Human, bird or stone?

The leaves sound like you;
You're every patch of green,
Every icy sunrise,
Every last standing tree.

So, is it you or them,
Whose voice echoes on concrete?
Do we tap your name?
Do we run to them?

And if you are the same,
Is it right to heed the calls?
Is it right to keep a garden?

Songs

Open Road

Open road,

Pine trees,

Cigarettes,

Sunburnt knees.

Your voice fuels the car

For miles and miles

And there's no turning back.

We're runners,

We're roamers,

We're children of the road.

There is no last stop;

Freedom's all we're after.

Old songs,

Bird calls,

Ocean waves,

No iron bars.

Your voice, the only guiding star

For miles and miles,

No turning back.

We're runners,

We're roamers,

We're children of the road.

There is no last stop;

Freedom's all we're after.

We roll along;

We chase the dawn.

On the road, we hide;

On the road our love's alive.

Open road...

Pine trees...

Cigarettes...

Green Wind

No home but the greenery;
No lover but open sky.
Our only wish is to live free;
Our curse, needing the high.

The road is long;
The night is young;
Our feet are strong;
We're already drunk.

No friend but your memory;
No regret but time wasted.
Betrayal is fuelling me;
The pines say chase it.

No point in goodbye;
We go where the wind blows.
Our curse is needing the high
Of going where no one goes.

Still

Silence reigns in the pine trees;

The wind blows cold

And carries only a quiet voice.

The lake is still;

Time rests on its waters,

Swaying in the winter air.

No other sound;

No eyes around.

The end of the road;

The end of the race.

In lasting peace

Without fear or rush,

Hill hides fool;

Dances over the abyss.

The end of all roads;

Us in the green.

We belonged to the mountain

Before you planted addiction on our feet.

Chimneys & Trees

The forest adores you,

But you're made of smoke.

The rocky cliffs lay hidden

Behind a smirk and a joke.

Green eyes light the way;

Foxes follow your step;

Flowers turn to your gaze,

Make your face bright red.

You're the song of the hills

Sung among buildings.

And I get chills

'Cause somewhere you're breathing.

Your voice shakes the ground;

Your whispers reach the birds.

The forest's awake with sound;

The green god is home.

Green eyes light the way;

The foxes follow your step;

Flowers turn to your gaze,

Make your face bright red.

You're the song of the hills

Sung among buildings.

And I get chills

'Cause somewhere you're breathing.

The abyss

Waits behind a full smile.

The abyss

Echoes the silent lines.

Chaos

Smoking on my doorsteps

Was Pan;

The wicked do not sit still.

We left;

The only way to go was up;

They knew.

We went beyond the road

And on;

Got so lost, I made a home

Afield.

Smoke Trees

Roadies —

Beyond all the roads.

Loners —

Home is the motion.

No good —

Chasers of the wild.

Too good —

Addicted to desertion.

This is the answer.

Roamers —

Beyond all known maps.

Stoners —

High on disruption.

Bad wood —

Meant just for burning.

Smoke wood —

Choking on rebellion.

Woodland Wind

Woodland god,

Dancing on,

You don't know the joy you spread.

Lonely in

The high crowd,

Joker, fool,

You don't know the load you bear.

Behind the boughs,

But your eyes shine through.

Laughing at the heavens,

Too tired to explain;

Jumping into lake

To shock-freeze the pain.

Child of the harsh woods,

Your song moves the earth

And comforts other fools.

Fool, you don't know the hills' pride.

Runner, are you free?

Roamer, do you rest?

Joker, will you laugh?
River, will you stop?

Do the trees look out for you?
Does the road ease your mind?
In your dancing, don't forget
Your worshiping high crowds.

Stuck

We live in the forest
Because that is where the road ended.

The piper lives in motion,
Knows where to go,
Knows the way,
Understands.

We breathe in trees and cars,
Picture the dance,
Look to the moon,
Cry at her and the summer stars.

Sky Reflection

On the way of pine trees
To the bottom of the hill,
No rest for you and me;
Glass can't hold us still.

Hear the people of the town;
We're the people of the road —
We don't sit on chairs,
We don't walk on stones.

But you see green,
Where it doesn't grow.
You let chimneys breathe;
We fell the willow,
We flood the scene.

See the houses built in rows;
We're living down on the dirt —
We don't talk at screens,
We don't stare, don't know.

But you see green,
Where it doesn't grow.

Owl

The mountaineer will come to rest under the old oak,
Who blocks the wind,
In the timeless heart of the forest,
Where time is slow.

Only the bark is really there;
The world is softly lit.
You will whisper lies to yourself,
That only the tree will hear.

The road will be far behind;
Your boots will have given in.
The campfire has taught you,
Your home is the lake's old oak tree.

Long Way

We never stopped for the trees,
But every path leads here.

In the clouds where you dug a hole,
The woods are dead.
We see the mountain fading
From the old oak's canopy.

Disruption may be
In that old tree,
Wherein lives, too, the forest's purity.
Even you would agree,
There is no more to see.

After mountains and smoke,
After fireworks and rain,
After wilderness and peace,
The road ends at the old oak,
Where, blue, festering, and aching,
We lay and weep.

Evergreen

Roots deep in the lake,

Blossoming in shade,

The lilies you smelled

Sigh their solitude away.

They share with the dark waters

The ghost of gentle strides,

Lighter than air,

Swifter than the current.

A spot chosen after much choosing

Of wrong words and layered lies;

Found after the long drive

From the edges to the tops the world.

There, over branches and petals,

The wind echoes your swan song:

'See you.'

Nett

We keep riding
On your trail,
Listening to the calypso drums
Of early mornings by the Salz.

Us, the small,
Us, from the edge,
We fit anywhere —

Somewhere new
Every three weeks.

We will return to our own hill,
Where the oaks await

To join you in breathing in
The tree-top sweet world.

Nothing II

I scream into the abyss to whisper in your ear;

We smoke in silence to bare our sins;

We dance to music only we hear;

You sing to your hills.

Mirror

Let the rain wash all that's green;

Fill our lungs;

Put out the smoke

Pray to those waters;

The torrents are our half;

The race's end.

Calls

We went to the mountains to forget ourselves.

Our madness is not our own;

Only the hills know.

And maybe the car.

And maybe the rain.

My go…

Your go…

Air

When you opened your hands,

The sun shone through your eyes.

When you flew over the void,

You wore the summer

On your Christmas jumper.

We tie the tails of your ribbons

To the flickers of a campfire;

Walk the universe you bear in arms.

And new songs

Travel only in the missed turns

Of your car.

Midtown

Pan plays softly;

The trees turn green.

The race will not end in smoke,

Or at a dead oak's stomp,

Or at the lake,

Or at sea,

Or at all.

It turns to a walk –

The runaways, wanderers,

The edge of the forest, a stop on the road.

The whistle is answer and call.

Litir

Forest for miles;
Can't get them back.
Forest for miles;
Can't turn around.

Where the car drove,
My legs can walk.
Where you danced,
I can sit and watch.

Back then, the lake was alight for the holidays;
Now it's wedding time on the boardwalk.
Yet, we were always there alone.
And I am still always there alone.

Where the train stops,
We can find our own way.
Where you grieved,
The cliffs sing your song.

Firefly

I am there,

Smoking off your hands,

In the blue,

In the tired, hollow bark,

On the two-seater;

The only sound is our laughter.

You're here,

In my house,

Dragging in the mountain.

Good that one of us is quiet.

We're there,

Afloat,

Burning winter clothes,

But stuck in the blue.

Aquarium

The river is the forest;

It flows in her arms;

It lives in everything —

Infinite, scattered, undefined,

Full of faces, scents, touches,

Cherished collection that cannot be held.

The wind comes, hits, caresses, leaves, plays with the water;

The river breathes it in through the trees,

Runs it to the sea, does not stop to ask,

It reaches all, holds all, becomes all along the way,

A never-ending stream of brief encounters.

It runs, sweeps, is swept;

Each breath adds to flow —

No stops for the living,

No stops for the running,

No stops for the scattered.

On Salvation

Mountain nights;

Packing for uphill climbs.

When your return is due,

Will the summer bring us edelweiss?

Will the roamers turn the tide twice?

Trapped in an old race,

Dancing to an old tune,

When the day is new,

Will we stop the fumes?

Will we the rocking chair embrace?

Quiet

Filled the woods with tenderness,

Covered the meadows in poetry,

Made a home in the green,

Where the road turns to pebbles,

To hear the pipes from the hills,

To keep chasing the sitting fool,

The beginning and end.

Prayers from the Rain

Green Smoke

In the cold forest,

The moon hidden,

Campfires fight the night

With quiet, gentle flames,

Comfort the frosted boughs,

Remind the wind of spring,

Teach the young of warmth.

Beauty and peace

Sleep on the hands of disruption;

As the campfire burns in the cold woods,

All moving things find their pace.

Even hiding, the moon knows

From the smoke,

And the hope in all the living,

That there was warmth where the cold wind blows,

And the forest shall again be green.

Backseat

Parked in the shadows,

Playing soft tunes,

Humming with the night —

Grasshoppers outside;

The mountain is ours,

So are the fumes,

So are the sighs.

Terrace

Gold-plated North coast,

On your sand, lie the pines.

From your cliffs, I look to Eire;

Under your sunlight, the wind cuts most.

Take away the forest and the fire,

But bring me back to Virginia.

Ten

Raindrops on my window;
You know what that means.
Here's the tropical shadow
Of winter's homely peace.

Every three weeks, it rains;
Here's the travelling moon.
You're wise to pack flames
For, at home, we dine at noon.

The skies pour until dawn
From hands onto ground.
Here's the frolicking fawn;
You know we will be found.

Slow dance

In the thickest woods,
Life goes slow —
The river is a lake;
Birds sing softly.

In the deepest woods,
Days are the same;
The breeze is still;
The waters, tame.

There is no road to where no one goes.
Plod through or stay.
To climb these hills,
Cuts take too long.

Where the woods grow tight,
Time stays out;
The sun is gentle;
The lake is warm;
No hills so high.

Where the woods are dark,
Day blends with night;
The river takes rest;

All roads die;

Luck leads the hike.

There is no road to where no one dares to go.

Plod through or stay.

To climb these hills,

Cuts take too long.

The Light

We laughed at the landscape.

The line is the cold light

Of our burning souls;

The edge is the fading smoke

Above the canopies.

We danced on their porches.

To us, peace moves fast

But not toward the hills.

They wait for the roses;

We run after lilies.

Hikers

Wild things —

We don't plan;

We don't stop;

We don't go back.

Our roads never meet.

But the mountains scream

Ever louder as we run.

We hear them awake;

They fill our dreams.

Runaways on top of the world,

Mountain chain sunrises,

Smoke and mist entwined,

Dark tattoos, light petals on grass,

Lulled and woke in the green;

Lungs full of each other's pain,

Riding the high of escape.

Please, tell your hills you're fine,

Keep them out of your days,

And let me go on with mine.

Let me breathe in other shades;

Let me run my own way.

Cold Night

Everyone knows the woods are cursed.

Everyone knows the moon is watching.

We know there is no point in dreaming.

We know poets will not sing the lost.

What the moon pulls in, she draws back.

What the moon reveals, she hides again.

In the sun, the trees are quiet and plain.

In the sun, our steps return to the trail,

Choosing home over novelty;

Choosing peace over the abyss.

You learn once,

You learn best.

The moon is watching the cursed.

Rivers II

There isn't enough about the river and its children
Because they are hard to keep track of.
But the forest knows them.
They trust the bed that protects them;
In their race, they are earthbound;
The leaves carry their voices —
They are as free as the roots they feed.

Static II

Moon and trees hold their breath
While lightning and water
Sense each other in dance.
They wait in wakeful silence
For thunder to return river to sea.

Then it storms in the forest,
Promising a shock-cleanse;
The river longing for the sea,
And the quiet reign of the moon
Over the dance of water and energy.

Rivers III

The rivers meet at the lake,

Slow each other's race,

Blend for your sake

And flow with gentle grace.

They stretch at leisure all day.

Time borrows their pace.

Waters of green and blue and grey

Swell, flood, embrace.

All

     is

          done;

              the

          ri-

     vers

won.

The Lake

Drowned in green,

The lake overflowing,

No current pulling,

Inked pipes blowing.

Drowned in poetry,

Left with words,

Facing the stars,

Tracing Mercury.

A storm at sea

Never to fall —

Restless clouds,

Gone the birds,

Gone the flies.

The lake fills,

The pipes sing:

'We leave in green.'

Campfire

The river flows gently by the campfire.
The crack of flames fills the night.
The moon touches all.
The smoke is in all breathing things.
Water and flames move in time,
Dream of the same end,
Look up at the same call.

Week by week

We only take one-way roads;
That's how we wound up in the forest,
Under the protection of the canopies
With filtered light and rain-
Ever the rain.

We only take first-time trails;
That's how we found the dream lake,
Hearing only the mountain's song
With hints of festival blues-
Ever the blues.

Frost

The wind of the mountain,

The wind of the sea

Are the smoke we drown in,

The voices we heed.

There is always another road to another hill;

We keep taking it.

We never say things as they are;

We stare at trees as at the light;

We live on the hill and get lost in fields for the love of you;

We are mad.

We, fools, know,

As the moon and the mountain know,

As the runners and the rivers know,

That there is nothing more than trees,

That only birds have it their way,

That their calls are not summons.

By the fireside the forest is not real —

The night, the moon are gone.

By the patient flames we can

See ourselves,

Feel our limbs.

We run to the mountain
To die by the campfire
By the madness and mercy of the smoke.

Lesson in White

Moon and campfire know everything that needs knowing;
Heard the thunder laugh before the storm;
Knew the dance before you twirled into the room.
Do not ask wild lilies to speak for you.
No one comes back from the hills.
Our feet run on betrayal.
In the mountains,
We smoke up
The void.

Beginning and End

I write about the forest
And not about us.
Though the forest lives in our shoes,
Of our soul there is nothing to tell —
Air, smoke, home.
I do not write about you —
We are but your long-lost bones,
And very last forgiving thoughts.
You, the valley we fit into,
The last thread of sanity,
The last trace of purity.
I write about the mountain,
But we hope to live
To dance at its feet.

Edges

We, from the edges of the world,
Carry the abyss in our chests.
Cold wind and storm clouds,
Had to jump off from her backseat
To land dumb on grass and nothing.

Dumb,
Listening to Dylan on repeat;
Dumb,
Living in the car… and naming her;
Dumb,
As all other racers and chasers.

We inhale that great beauty,
Rolled in silence and poetry.
Another song before dinner,
A dumb one for the road.

Beams

The road never leads to the field of golden blossoms;

You don't wander far from the shadows of the mother's woods;

We are far enough from the shore.

Deep green doesn't blend with the yellow feast;

We have our own rain dance,

Our own breed of joy —

Bright ribbons hanging from the car.

We smile at the abyss,

Never at the sun.

Never Apart

The mountain, only, knows the pain of the happy piper;

The mountain, only, can comfort the fool.

Though our foolishness is quieter, we run to the mountain, too.

No such green, except the trees;

The trees, only, know that soul;

The trees, only, can claim it;

To the trees, only, it returns.

Though our silence is sadder, we run to the trees, too.

Riders

It's not about the lake.

All the mountain's rivers,
All the mountain's roads

Lead

To

Sea.

It's not about the lake.

As all sea waves curl,
As all sea waves pull

Fool

To

Moon.

Going uphill
Is not about the push,

It is about the fall.

Driving away

Is not for the promise,

It is for the betrayal.

We never came back from the woods;

The bushes are not done consuming us,

Or we, climbing against the cold wind.

On your tracks, dark fool,

Flowers bloom and sing your name;

On mine, the smoke from your last pack.

And, on their ears, the cliffs echo

Our screams and laughter,

The live burning of sun chasers,

The drowning of hearts at sea,

The burial of souls under rocks.

Prayers from the City

Once

We run out to the green

To run out to you,

But there is little solace in the city —

Parks and cars are a faint ghost

Of your scent of trees and smoke.

Swim across lake,

Lay in the grass,

Smile and stare,

Run uphill,

Make a mess,

Dance around us,

Fly above our heads,

Curse,

Drive us,

Take our breath.

You are in everything;

Your pieces cannot be grasped.

Like me,

You are slippery.

You and I leave only trails

And they never cross.

We don't rest;

The hills won't let us —

Ever their travelling fools.

We live in the cold wind,

We carry smoke and trees,

And sense each other in the cold air.

Fireheart

Without the moon,

Breathe in the fool,

Open the way to the jokester.

On the trail of the pure,

The earthen voice of the mountain

Screams the truth.

The answer is always in the spinner,

In the owner of the wild woods and wild parties,

In the driver of fast cars and fast harvests,

In the one who wears joy as a borrowed Sunday suit,

And brings the depths of the edge out for drinks

In the moonlight.

Thyme

Moonlit hillside blues;
Anything but stuck.
Moonlit roadside blues;
Anything but parked.

Sanity grows on trees;
Madness on fingertips;
Dreams from whispers;
Speed from kisses.

Don't look for it,
Don't pray for it —
Wishes burn fuel.

Sense

Every night was the night.

Ditched the car for the train;

The city returned us to the mountain.

Played our stories on the 5 am stage.

It all comes down to the moment

That we read the right lines.

It all comes up to you and I,

Standing alone under the trees.

Every day is the day

That we will quit.

Summers

Sitting in a park,

Pretending it's the forest,

Breathing in the green and grey,

We speed down the mountain,

Feeling you before meeting you,

Plunging into the green,

On the verge of a fatal fall,

Fear just beneath our skin.

It was the beginning and the end;

It was the call we never stop heeding.

First, landed on grass,

Now, aching for the hills.

Years will weigh on that handshake

And nothing will be left of it,

And never again will we meet,

But runners cannot stop.

Our feet will always find the forest,

Chase the hill's light, voice, and smell.

Even sitting between walls,

The mountain will keep us running.

Beneath

Back to the trees;

Tell me what to do

About the city questions,

About the death row walks.

What we knew was the mountain top;

What we knew was the lake's bottom.

Back to the trees;

Tell me what to answer

To the bonfire's sweet glow

When we are but green drops;

When we are but green fog.

Runners

All our escapes belong to you.

You invented them and sowed into us.

We won't meet,

We won't part.

See, we are like you —

We, too, love the Earth.

We run to the forest to breathe;

We heed only to the whispers of water and leaves.

Always far, always worth the journey,

So, we don't stop —

We get lost,

We chase oblivion through the trees,

We never rest;

That's the closest we can get to peace.

Hoping the road will be done;

Dreaming of a home on the ground,

Of living off pines and fog,

Of catching up with the eve.

Quiet Flutes

The road is empty.
The woods thrive in silence.
We missed the ride,
But walk the tyre tracks.
We look through glass
With only memories and songs for protection.
Walking, we still follow the pipes.
The moon understands;
She knows how we would dance.
Alas, we walk
Through silent woods.

Cravings

The cold wind learned about summer,
Roasting pine nuts with a coconut thief.
Fire out, the mountain smells of peace;
Swinging, trunks call to the sea.
Riding over the abyss on a rosemary leaf,
Roamer ensnared roamer.
Road gone, the hill smells of belief;
Fools freed, the wind craves the sea.

Retro

The blossoms:

The widow who paints only in green;

Your mother texting like your hidden lover;

The undefeated blushing over a chessboard.

The writers:

The mother won't save your kind;

Your house decays like your walking shoes;

Your god sleeps on a tyrant's bed.

The runners:

Your date wants lectures;

Your friends leave like you did;

A lily sleeps under an old oak tree.

Bears

In the sounds of the forest,
There are no songs or lies;
No one is smuggled into the meadow;
No one cares if you smile.

Silent is the remaining mist
Of an unresolved mountain tale,
Dead at the hands of a hiker,
Who rides through its drops.

Too far beyond the road;
Have long left our shoes behind.
Weary, we step on rocks and mud going nowhere.
The grunting beast will be our fellow.

Green & Neon

Headlights at 2.00 a.m.,

Rushing to the lake,

Picked a cigarette from under the seat,

Picked a lily from under the old oak tree,

Threw my boots over the fence.

Rivers drag everything in their path.

Something about that lake makes everything miss it.

Empty night bus at 3.00,

Running to someone's house,

Picked the guitar too late to leave,

Picked take out under neon signs,

Helped my polka dots into the bar.

Hills sing over amplifiers and trance.

Something about the scene makes everyone quit it.

Laendler

I cried today because I saw home when the man asked the way.

The same way I did when you said your piece over walls and lines,

And on the day when your old jumper got you coffee and pardon.

Did the offbeat walk to hide behind a glass of water;

The wildfire self-consumed in trying not to burn his fines;

The silence rolled off your one suit and bare fingers.

Again, the tongue split and couldn't taste;

Again, the air failed and spoken words hit;

Again, we stepped on the plane.

Where it goes

Everyone hears the city in your voice,

The smoke in your laughter,

The pine needles of your French,

But only I break down.

The ride is silent, but it's alright,

When in the business of speeding downhill,

We all end up in the black lake

With or without the monk's laundry.

The waters will wash the mud from our shoes,

The forest will welcome us home,

And, somehow or another,

There will be beer in our cups, stew our bowls,

And music to protect us from the darkness.

You said there aren't many like me in the wild,

So I followed your trail and went there.

You're not here, but I want to stay,

'Cause I saw the end and know it well —

Alone at the end of all roads;

Alone in the care of your hills;

Alone, defeated, and singing.

Lumps

You left boxes of goodbyes
And walked off
Into the wild.

We flooded the void with green
And moved on
Into the lights.

We cut the party with silence
And go through
Into the sea.

Met in our race
And ran our way,
Tied to the path.

If we found peace,
It smelled of smoke,
Of pines,
Of sea.

Breathless

Something is still wrong

Since driving up the mountains from the edge,

And starting the ride with goodbye.

Something will stay wrong,

As we wander the green vastness alone,

Hearing your mother's blessings in the cold wind.

Something is still incurable

In the fast runners stranded in foreign woods,

All the while longing for the moon herself.

Only weariness grows on our path,

And the tone of our hills' calls,

Cursing the day, we left.

Singing

Among ruins,

The loud chains of greetings,

The screaming rules of tapping

Resist.

The source of restlessness,

The stirrer of senses

Is too far to guide the pen.

Hide in poetry,

Throw frustration at the great smoky mountains,

Water the plants,

Hug the pines,

Run.

Roamer Blues

Small talk for relief;

A new lie every three weeks.

Ink, ink, ink,

And pinewood,

And the absence of longing.

We hug our trees,

We run to sea,

To the lakes,

To where cars never break down.

Road, road, road;

'See you,' sing the blessed,

Leaving heart-shaped boxes in the bushes,

Walking in

In anything.

Throw the chain down the cliff;

Heave, heave, heave;

Choke on green.

Lightness

You say the word;

Trails part for you.
No matter
That we only come to the hills to get lost.
There are no drums or strings in the forest;
No matter —
The oak listens.

We make the face;

The city is closed.
No matter —
Fuel is never a problem for smokers.
There will be mirth and screams in the forest;
No matter —
The road is open.

No matter, we run;
No matter, we return;
No matter, we dance.

Slippery

You don't see many of our kind on city streets,

Shaking hands with green,

Under a new tree every week,

Laying on new ground,

Sensing other roamers;

Always too fast except for flowers,

Always too loud except for ourselves.

Only in rivers lives the race,

That drags the earth with us

To a poster

Of the sea.

Racing

The trouble is
Fools find fools
In the depths of the woods.

The trouble is
Trouble is not
In the depths of the woods.

Week by week,
We come back
To tell lies,
Do laundry,
Fill the tank,
Steal a pack.

The trouble is
Roamers.
The trouble is
Rivers.
The trouble is
Rest.

Pipers

Got lost in the hills
In a car with the forest's son,
Dancing behind the wheel,
Speeding over cliffs.

Got lost in the city lights
Through the electric one's
Camera eyes,
Dancing behind wires,
Laughing between shifts.

Got lost with the pipers;
Never once left the ocean,
Never learned to breathe,
Never lost our fright.

Walk

I come to the mountain top to shout at you.

Jump back on into the jalopy.

You are no freer than me;

We are no freer apart.

There are only so many roads;

There are only so many trees.

We are both of the ocean;

We are both of the tides;

Neither can hold or be held;

We float and sway,

And wait,

And wish for the wind to land us on leaves,

And smoke fear outside.

Darlings

This is to say, we are lost,
Lost and loose.
I ride still on your passenger seat;
Careful what you wear to your dreams;
Careful what you eat at your doom;
We still ride on your mother's push.

Roamers, wisemen,
Road and rest are right here,
In the smoky car, in the wild woods,
In the wild rides, in the smoky streams,
Right here are home and health.
This is to say we are saved,
Saved and crazed.

Circles

Ghost body sensing

The wrong turn…

The wild are hard to find;

On every spin, rest the mad.

Breaking for the thrill

Tins, spoons, spirits.

No dash can help fear;

No pull can hold runners.

Willingly

Ran crazy uphill,

Waltzed on the table;

The trees still talk of that spring.

Followed the thrill,

Got on the plane;

The rain now plays violin strings.

Patience

The race is lost,

But trees grow back;

And grass, behind your step.

Forget what we forgot;

Runners will walk.

When all is gone,

We sit by the lakeside.

We climb to the top

With ribbons in arms;

We're bringing it back-

Col agus craic.

Let it take years;

Let us dry;

Let it be spring.

Chokes

Let unyielding trees die screaming;

A mountainside hearth silently hit by a train.

How do you talk to the rest of your life?

Asks a fire flint who never once lived.

The wind knows laughing is devilish.

Why must one be still?

Blues and prayers don't travel;

Toys don't return from the woods,

As flagged cars run only at night,

As greatness dissolves in lakes,

As grass pulls everything down.

When the wall breaks, is it your skull?

Hum and buzz aloud at the stars!

Scream, laugh, grab your guts for the last time!

Shotgun into the abyss for the tenth time!

How do you save your heart from the raging ocean,

Floating on your reflection and old furniture?

The rain is never alone, never water, never cold;

Let screamers die in peace.

Aesthete

Shouting at all we hated,

We smudged leaves,

Stroke the wrong chords.

And the band you never told me about?

Are they better than you?

I cannot break the you-and-birds diet.

Get off the bus

With the guitar and winter jumpers,

Not cringing or brewing,

Shouting at all we wanted.

The woods for a lamp!

I filled the rosy page,

And the mother's voice echoed.

Is it because of all our questions?

Hysteria is a laughing man.

The woods for a rainy day…

Get off the bus,

In the general direction of never again,

Shouting at all your father said.

We smoked the rosy page.

The Sea

Dancer and drummer,

We roam the forest

With driver and rider.

Let us die here among weeds,

Let us listen to the birds' waltz

Until only mist is left...

On the kitchen counter,

Master and seeker,

Alone;

Your clothes, blue and old;

Glasses,

We saw only each other;

And yet,

Words, missing.

Schedule

Forest nymphs walk beside us.

Week by week,

We climb.

One, two, dream,

One, two, dream…

Miles and miles,

We ride;

Only smokes in our pockets—

Heavy load,

Rotten air.

Morning, folks!

One, two, dream…

Night Star and New Moon

A ripple of disruption —
A low fire undoes winter
And burns softly in the green;
A night heals a lifetime
And relieves the neon sting;
A teacher leads the dance
And mends by breaking free
The greatness of small things,
The eternal beauty of brevity.

As the fools return to the hills,
Freedom does to green
To forget the blinding lights.

Goodbye to goodbyes.
Back to peace by the fireside;
Back to only watching the dance.
Fool, breath of all living things,
The green will be your presence.